Eric Clapton Style

Guitar Book with Online Video & Audio Access

Taught By
Jody Worrell

To Access Online Audio & Video for this course, go to the following web address:

http://cvls.com/extras/ecs/

Copyright 2017 by Watch & Learn, Inc., First Edition
ALL RIGHTS RESERVED. Any copying, arranging, or adapting of this work without the consent of the owner is an infringement of copyright.

The Author

Jody Worrell has been a professional performer and teacher in the Atlanta area for over 30 years. He has recorded and appeared on stage domestically and internationally with such artists as Lyle Lovett, Mitch Ryder and the Detroit Wheels, Badfinger, Delbert McClinton, Phil Collins, The Marvelettes, The Drifters, The Tokens, The Crystals, Derek Trucks, and many others. Jody plays all styles on demand, but always returns to the blues, taking an approach which is based in tradition, but always seeking to expand harmonic boundaries. He also has to his credit four of the many Watch & Learn products: *Let's Jam! CD Blues & Rock Vol. 3, Let's Jam! CD Country Vol. 2, Let's Jam! Blues Standards,* and *Blues Licks & Solos*.

Jody studied classical guitar briefly with the legendary John Sutherland, but attributes his playing mostly to hard work, open-mindedness to diverse types of music, and to the indelible mark left by long-time teacher, mentor and friend, Merrill Dilbeck. Jody has produced almost three hundred video lessons on blues, rock, and country for GuitarCompass.com.

How To Use The Book & Video

Step 1 - Watch the Video while following along with the book. Play along with the Video on your guitar. Replay each chapter on the Video until you are comfortable playing along with it.

Step 2 - When you are comfortable with a lesson or piece of music, try playing along with the audio track for each lesson. Try expanding your horizons a little and stretch out your technique. Don't be afraid to experiment.

Step 3 - Go back to the book & Video and play along to make sure you're on the right track.

If you have any questions, problems, or comments, please contact us:

Watch & Learn, Inc.
2947 East Point St
East Point, GA 30344
800-416-7088
sales@cvls.com

TABLE OF CONTENTS

	Page
Tuning, Tablature, & Techniques	5
Tuning	6
Relative Tuning	7
Tablature	8
Hammer-ons & Pull-offs	9
Slides & Bends	10
Classic Clapton Style Licks Part 1	11
Lick 1	12
Licks 2 & 3	13
Licks 4 & 5	14
Playing With Jam Track	14
Classic Clapton Style Licks Part 2	15
Lick 1	15
Licks 2 & 3	16
Licks 4 & 5	17
Playing With Jam Track	17
Eric Clapton Style Solo 1	18
Phrase 1	18
Phrases 2 & 3	19
Phrase 4	20
Whole Solo	20-21
Eric Clapton Style Solo 2	22
Phrase 1	22
Phrases 2 & 3	23
Phrase 4	24
Whole Solo	24-25
Clapton Style Solo In C 1	26
Phrase 1	26
Phrases 2 & 3	27
Phrase 4	28
Whole Solo	28-29
Clapton Style Solo In C 2	30
Phrase 1	30
Phrases 2 & 3	31
Phrase 4	32
Whole Solo	32-33
Where To Go Next	34

About This Course

Eric Clapton Style is the second installment in the *In The Style Of The Legends Series*. All courses include online Video & Audio Access packed full of famous licks and solos as interpreted by Jody Worrell. The courses are in the style of legendary guitarists such as Stevie Ray Vaughan, Eric Clapton, Jimi Hendrix, B.B. King and David Gilmour.

Each lick and solo is broken down and the techniques and timing of each phrase is totally explained and played several times. Close-ups and split screens are used to make learning even clearer. In addition to the video instruction, there are full band practice tracks allowing the students to practice with a professional band anytime they want to perfect their timing and technique.

A book is included with the Videos that has standard music notation and tablature for everything that is taught. The type face is large for ease of viewing.

The *In The Style Of The Legends Series* is based on content developed during 15 years of producing lessons for GuitarCompass.com which have been viewed by millions of guitarists. If you like these DVDs and want more high quality lessons, go to GuitarCompass.com to see our Free Lessons and Premium Lessons.

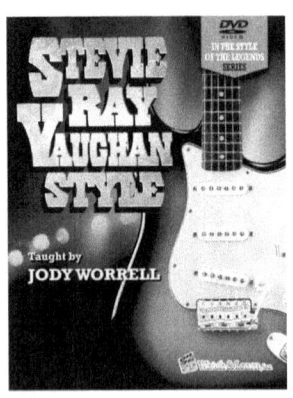   

To Access Audio & Video for this course, go to the following web address:
http://cvls.com/extras/ecs/

Gibson®, and the distinctive headstock design commonly found on Gibson® guitars, are registered trademarks of Gibson Guitar Corporation, and used herein with express written permission. All rights reserved.

TABLATURE & TECHNIQUES

To Access Audio & Video for this course, go to the following web address:

http://cvls.com/extras/ecs/

Tuning The Guitar

Before playing the guitar, it must be tuned to standard pitch. If you have a piano at home, it can be used as a tuning source. The following picture shows which note on the piano to tune each open string of the guitar to.

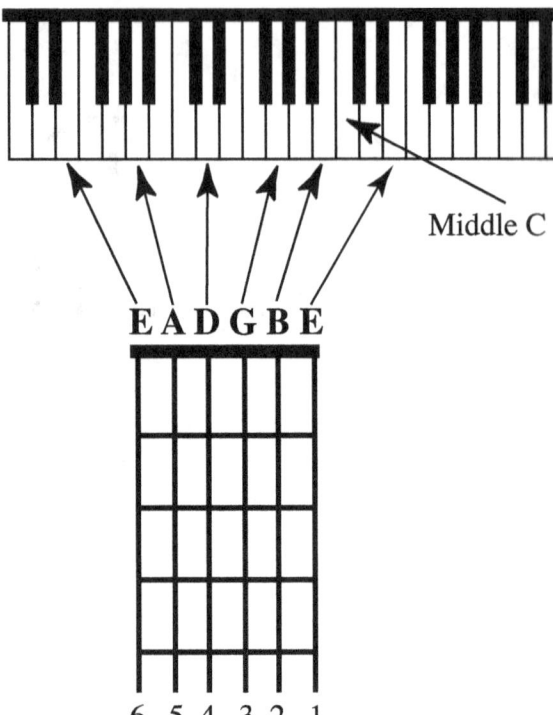

Electronic Tuner

An electronic tuner is the fastest and most accurate way to tune a guitar. We highly recommend getting one. They are available for $15 and up. Check with your local music store. You can also get an app for your smart phone.

RELATIVE TUNING

Relative tuning means to tune the guitar to itself and is used in the following situations:

1. When you do not have an electronic tuner or other source to tune from.
2. When you have only one note to tune from.

In the following example we will tune all of the strings to the 6th string of the guitar, which is an E note.

1. Place the ring finger of the left hand behind the fifth fret of the 6th string to fret the 1st note. Tune the 5th string open (not fretted) until it sounds like the 6th string fretted at the 5th fret.
2. Fret the 5th string at the 5th fret. Tune the 4th string open (not fretted) until it sounds like the 5th string at the 5th fret.
3. Fret the 4th string at the 5th fret. Tune the 3rd string open until it sounds like the 4th string at the 5th fret.
4. Fret the 3rd string at the 4th fret. Tune the 2nd string until it sounds like the 3rd string at the 4th fret.
5. Fret the 2nd string at the 5th fret. Tune the 1st string open until it sounds like the 2nd string at the 5th fret.

Now repeat the above procedure to fine tune the guitar. Until your ear develops, have your teacher or a guitar playing friend check the tuning to make sure it is correct.

The following diagram of the guitar fret board illustrates the above procedure.
Note - Old dull strings lose their tonal qualities and sometimes tune incorrectly.

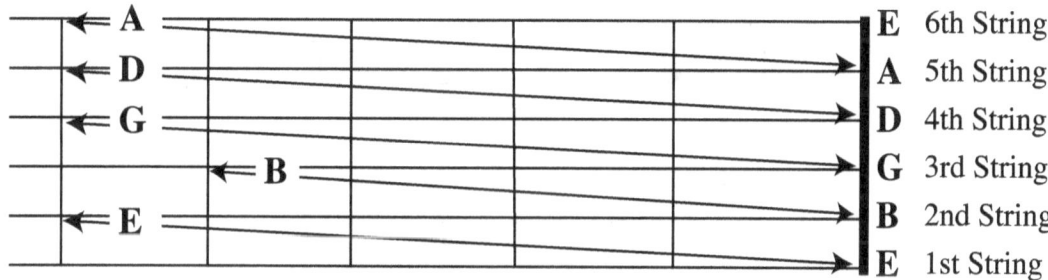

Check with your teacher or favorite music store to make sure your strings are in good playing condition.

TABLATURE

This book is written in both tablature and standard music notation. We will explain tablature because it is easy to learn if you are teaching yourself and because a lot of popular guitar music is available in tablature.

Tablature is a system for writing music that shows the proper string and fret to play. In guitar tablature, each line represents a string on the guitar. If the string is to be fretted, the fret number is written on the appropriate line. Otherwise a 0 is written. Study the examples below until you understand them thoroughly.

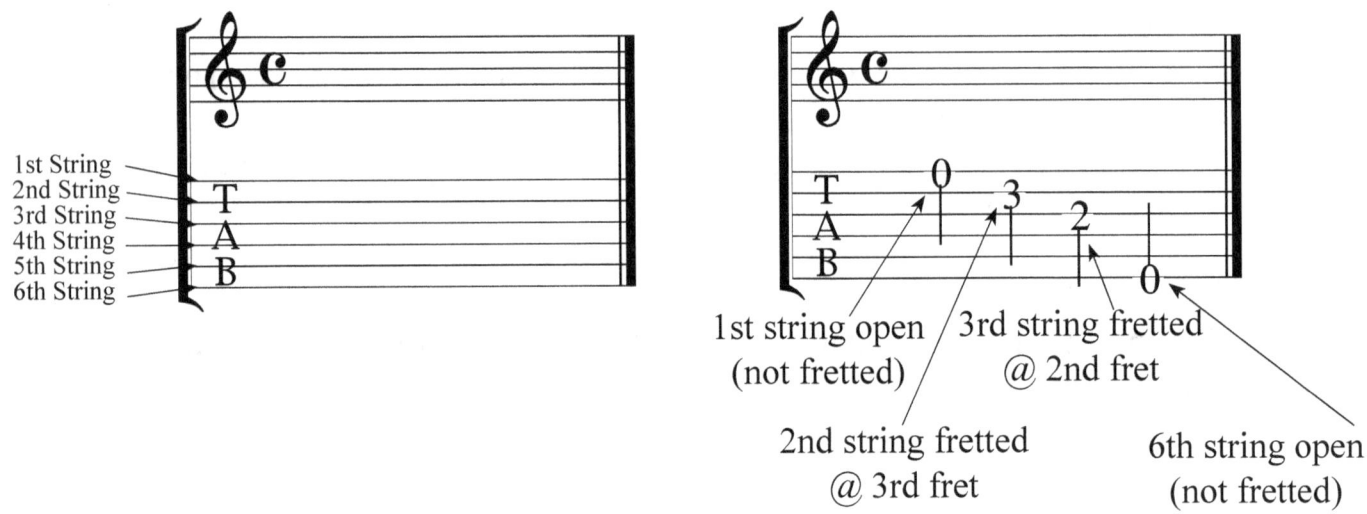

The music will be divided into two sets of lines (staffs).

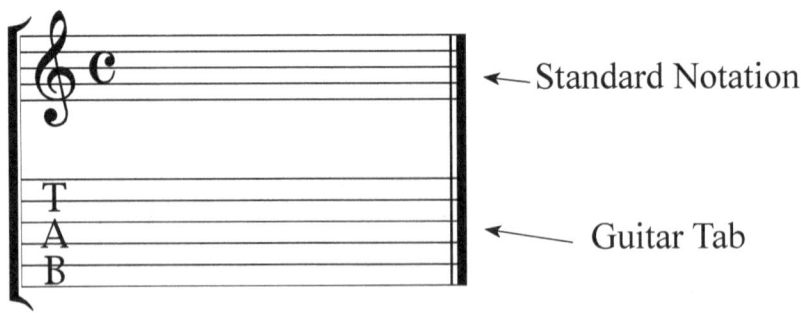

TECHNIQUES

Here are some fundamental techniques that are used this course.

Hammer-ons & Pull-offs

When playing a hammer-on, pick the first note, then hammer-on with a finger on your left hand. You will need to be on the tip of the finger and strike the note with velocity and accuracy.

When playing a pull-off, again pick the first note, then pull-off with a finger on your left hand. Once again, use the tip of the finger. The finger you are pulling off to needs to hold the string stable during the pull off.

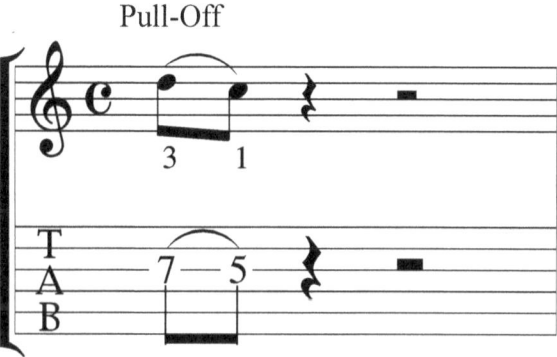

Hammer-on & Pull-off Combination

This technique starts by picking the first note, hammering on, and then pulling off back to the first note.

Slides

A slide means you pick a note and slide into another. Slides can move up or down and can be phrased many different ways.

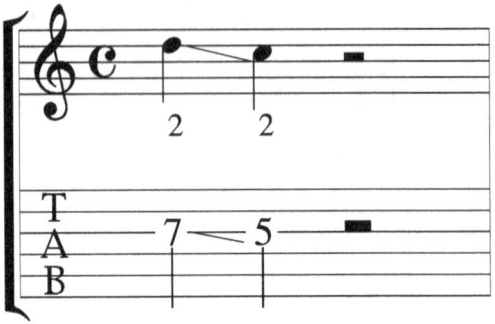

Slides From An Undetermined Note

This slide usually starts a fret or two away but sometimes further. It does not stay at the starting point long enough for the listener to really tell where it starts.

Double Stop Slides

This is a slide involving two notes. It is important that both fingers move evenly across the frets.

Bends

When playing a bend, use all the fingers that are available to help execute the bend. For example, use the third finger to bend the note, the second finger on the same string helping to bend the note, and the first finger to mute the string above it.

ERIC CLAPTON STYLE LICKS & SOLOS

To Access Audio & Video for this course, go to the following web address:

http://cvls.com/extras/ecs/

Classic Clapton Style Licks Part 1

We'll learn five licks in the style of Eric Clapton. We'll discuss some of his techniques, tricks, and note choices that have helped him establish his trademark sound. The Video will cover some of the music theory behind each lick as well as give you an opportunity to "trade" the licks back and forth in a jam situation. All of these licks are in the key of D and we'll focus on the D7 chord. We've included an audio track so you can practice these new ideas.

Lick 1

Start with a rest and then a hammer-on. Listen to the Video.

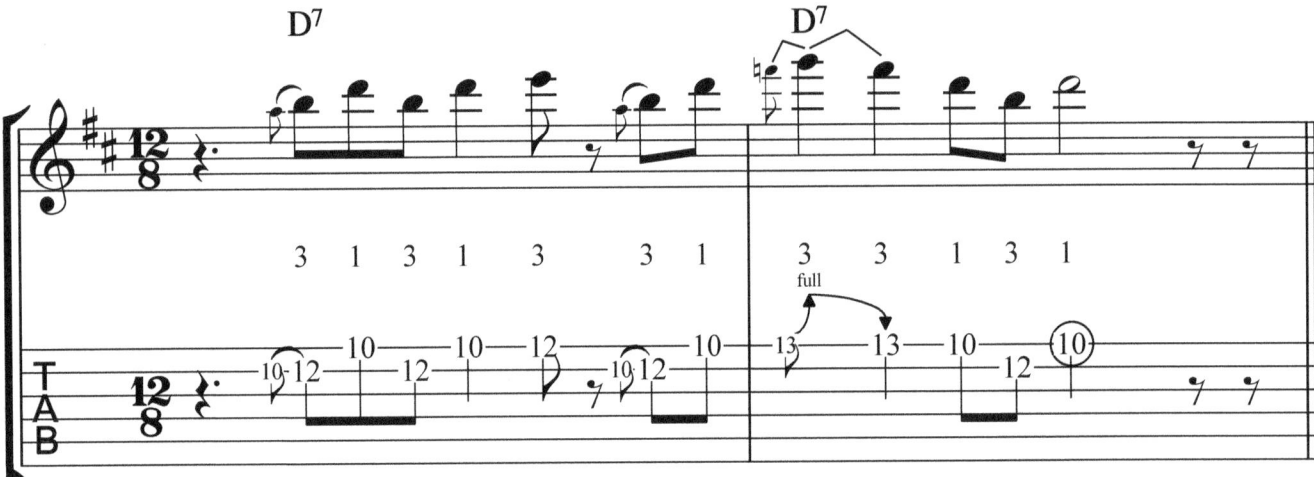

Demo

Each lick will be played along with a backing track at the correct speed.

Trading Licks

Each lick will be traded back & forth. I'll play it first, then leave space for you to play it right after so you can compare your tone, timing, and articulation. Take your time and work on this section until you can play it perfectly all three times.

Video & Audio Access

To Access Audio & Video for this course, go to this web address:
http://cvls.com/extras/ecs/

Lick 2

We'll use the same format for each lick. Each lick will be taught in detail. Next it will be played at full speed along with a backing track. Then it will be traded back and forth, leaving space for you to play right after me.

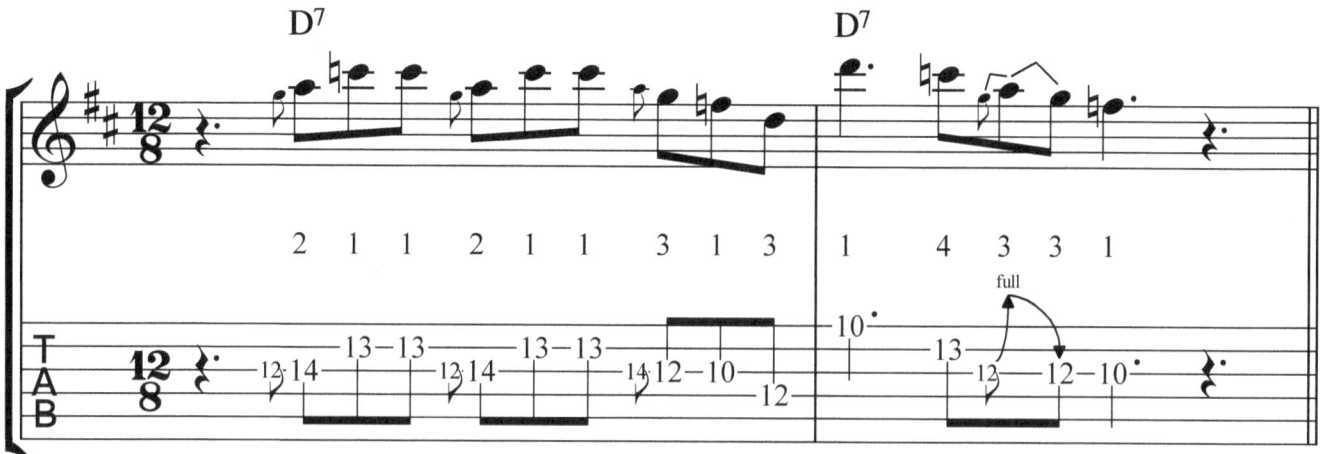

Lick 3

Lick 3 starts with a classic bending phrase.

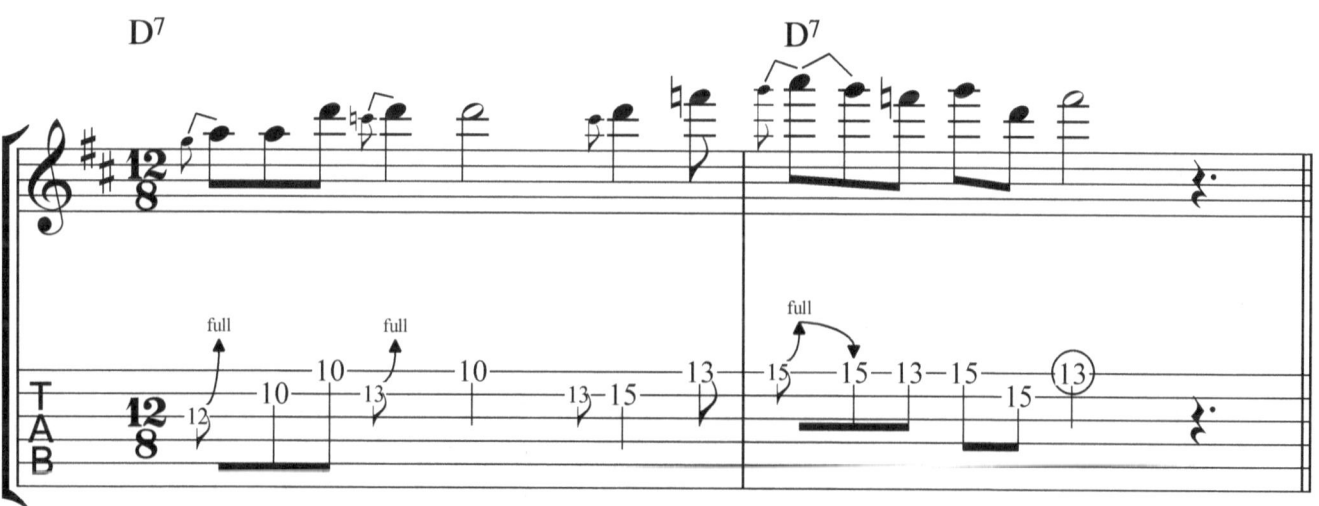

Note: You'll get the most from these lessons by taking your time and practicing each lick until you've mastered it. That's when you'll really be able to retain the licks and bring them into your day to day playing.

Lick 4

Start with the same three notes as in Lick 3.

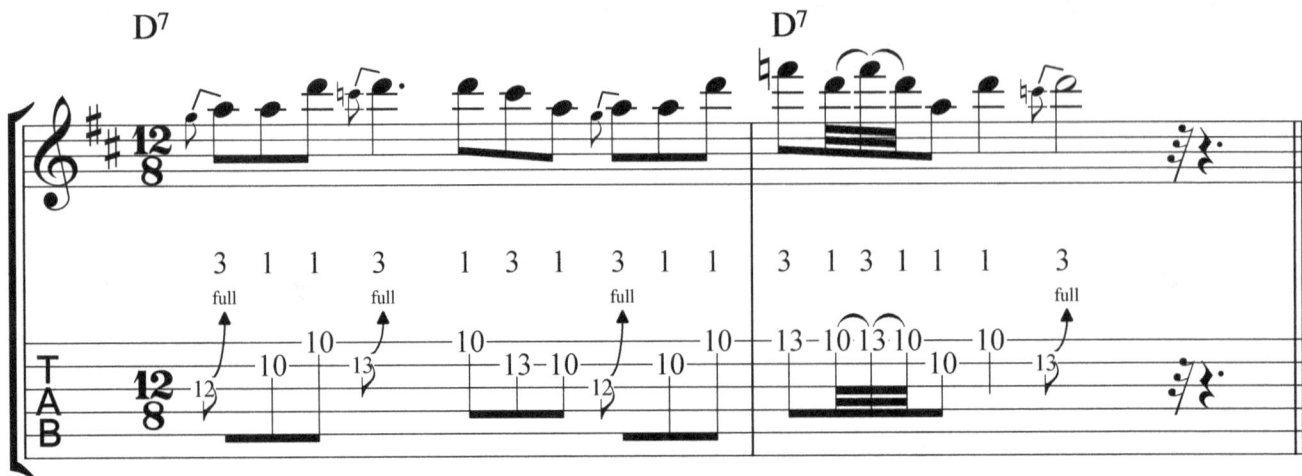

Lick 5

This lick starts with a phrase similar to Lick 2.

Playing With Jam Track

Now we'll play all five licks along with the audio track in a random order. When you get to the point where you can pick and choose them as you like, you're well on your way to owning the licks and you can use them in your day to day playing.

To practice along with just the audio track, you can access and download the file from the following web address:

http://cvls.com/extras/ecs/

Classic Clapton Style Licks Part 2

This lesson will look at another series of guitar licks inspired by Eric Clapton that focus on his trademark bends and slurs as well as his approach to tone. We'll cover each lick in detail by examining the techniques required to play the lick and the music theory behind it.

Lick 1

This lick starts with a hammer-on and then a bend & release.

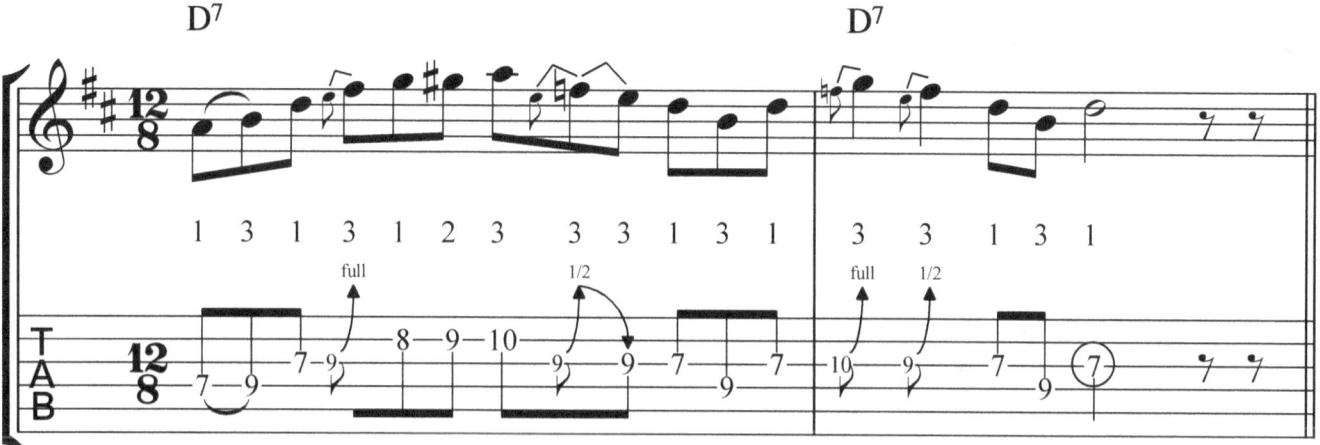

Demo

Each lick will be played along with a backing track at the correct speed.

Trading Licks

Each lick will be traded back & forth. I'll play it first, then leave space for you to play it right after so you can compare your tone, timing, and articulation. Take your time and work on this section until you can play it perfectly all three times through.

Video & Audio Access

To Access Audio & Video for this course, go to this web address:
http://cvls.com/extras/ecs/

Lick 2

This lick starts with a big bend & release at the 13th fret and then a hammer-on.

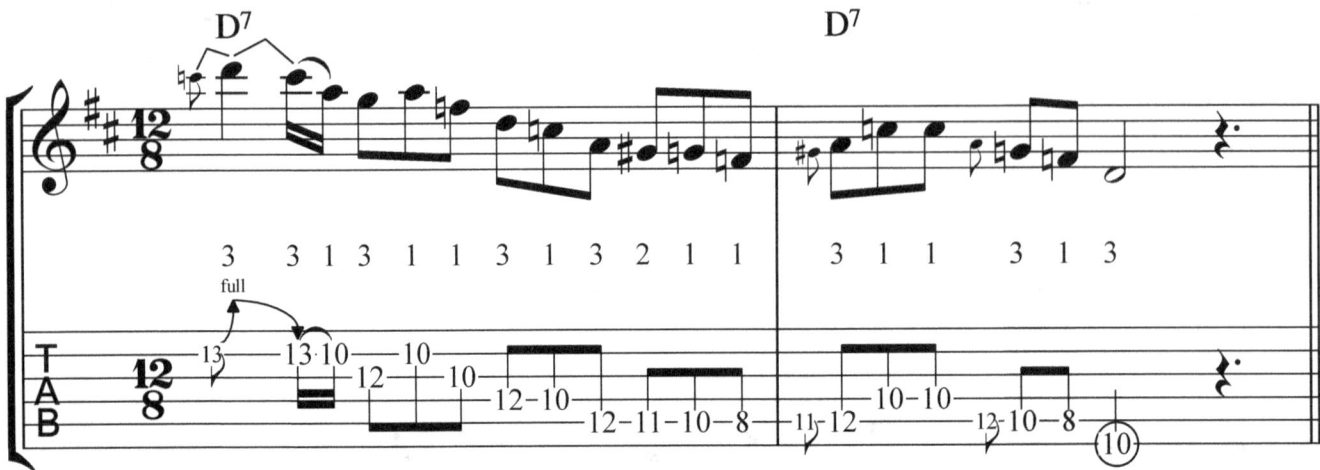

Lick 3

Start after a three beat rest with a full bend. This is all about controlling bends & releases and the length of notes.

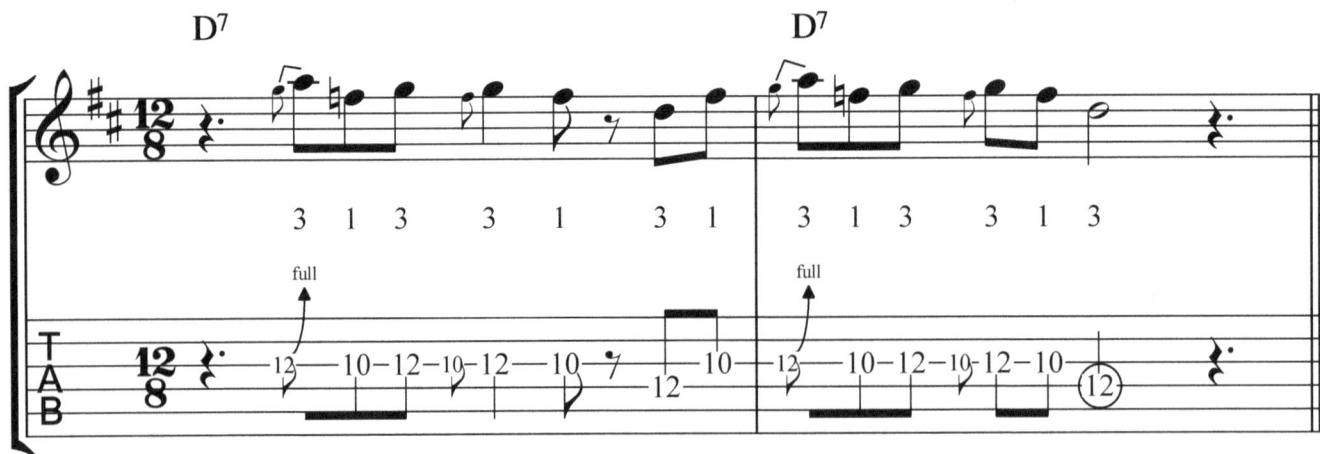

Note: Another great drill is to play the licks with me as well as in between in the trading section. Try this for all five licks in this section.

Lick 4

Again, start with a big bend at the 13th fret.

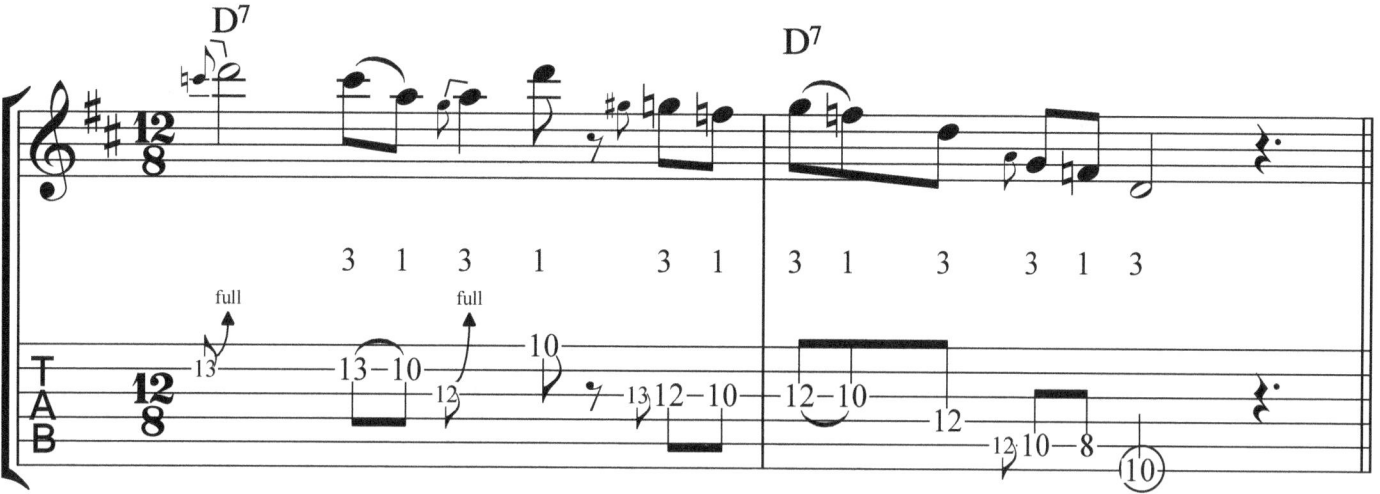

Lick 5

Start with a slight bend and mute.

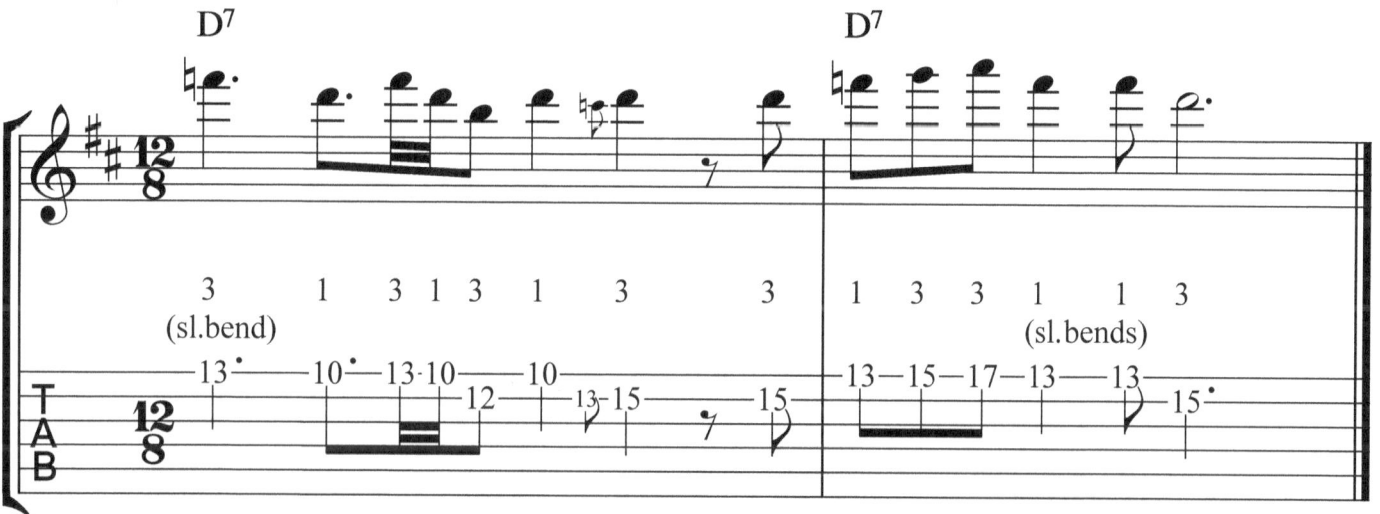

Playing With Jam Track

Now we'll play all five licks along with the audio track in a random order. When you get to the point where you can pick and choose them as you like, you're well on your way to owning the licks and you can use them in your day to day playing.

To practice along with just the audio track, you can access and download the file from the following web address:

http://cvls.com/extras/ecs/

Eric Clapton Style Solo 1

This lesson will teach you an 8 bar blues guitar solo in A and draws on Eric Clapton's inspired lead playing over a blues shuffle. I will teach you how to play each section of the solo while highlighting the techniques that gave Eric his unique sound. This solo is played over the *Key To The A Way* audio track from *Let's Jam! CD Blues & Rock Volume 3*. We will start by playing the complete solo along with the jam track and then break the solo into four phrases.

Phrase 1

Notice the quick bend and release in bar 2.

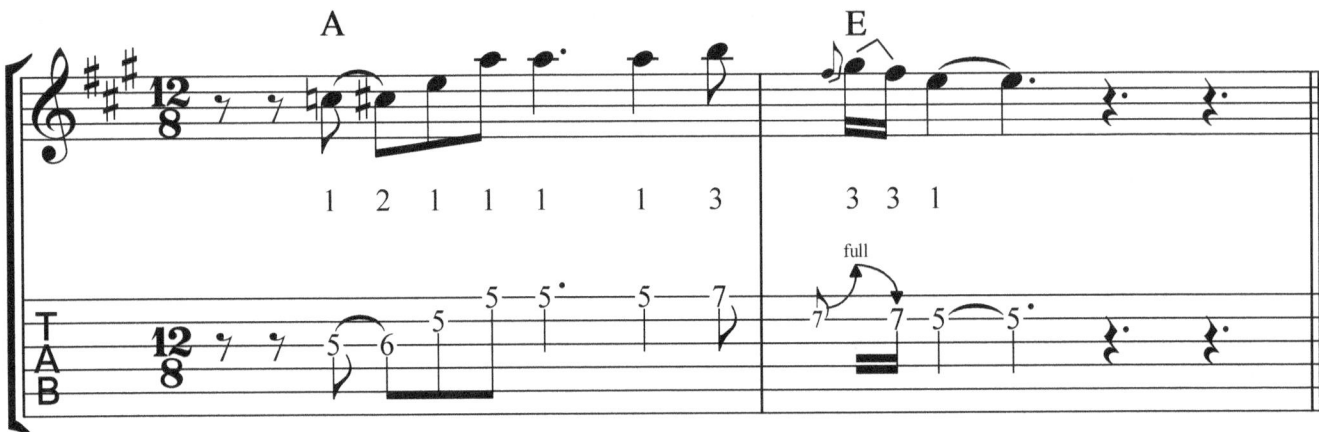

Demo

Each phrase will be played along with a backing track at the correct speed.

Trading Licks

Each lick will be traded back & forth. I'll play it first, then leave space for you to play it right after so you can compare your tone, timing, and articulation. Take your time and work on this section until you can play it perfectly all three times through.

Video & Audio Access

To Access Audio & Video for this course, go to this web address:
http://cvls.com/extras/ecs/

Phrase 2

Start with a bend at the 13th fret using either the 3rd or 4th finger.

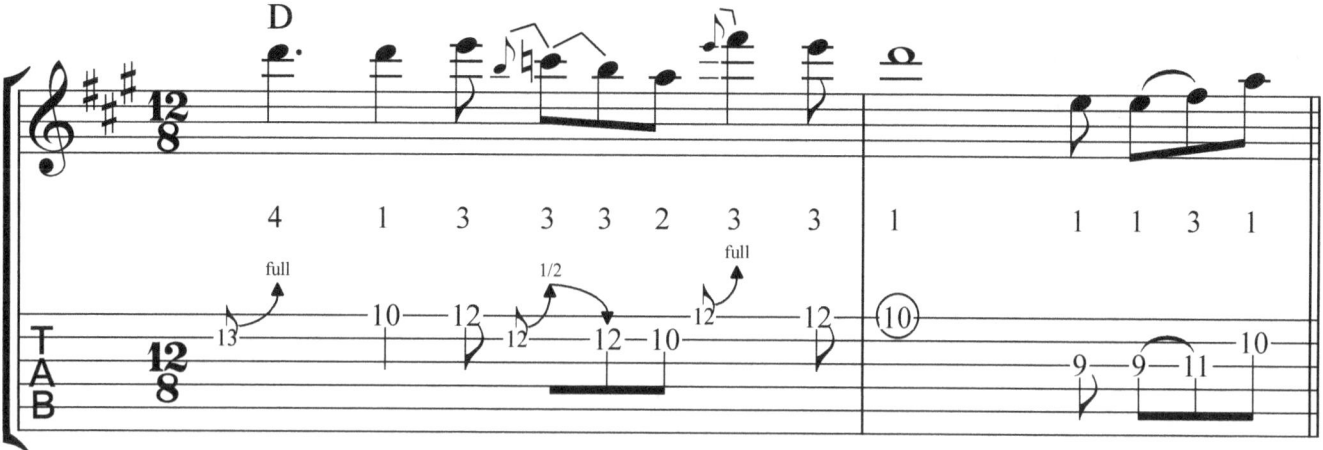

Phrase 3

The last four notes in Phrase 2 are pick up note for Phrase 3.

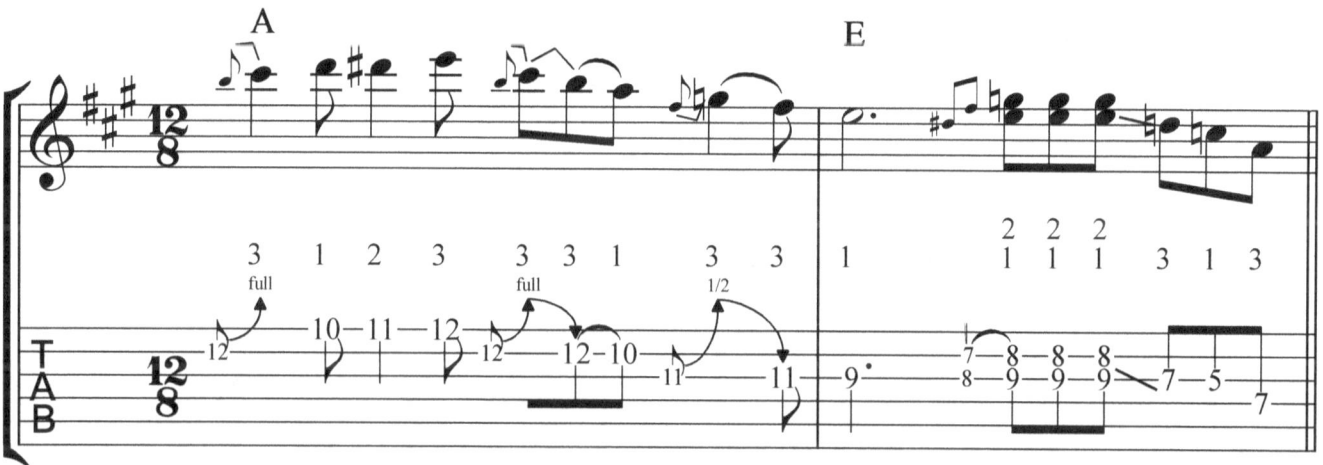

Phrase 4

This solo ends with a blues turnaround lick.

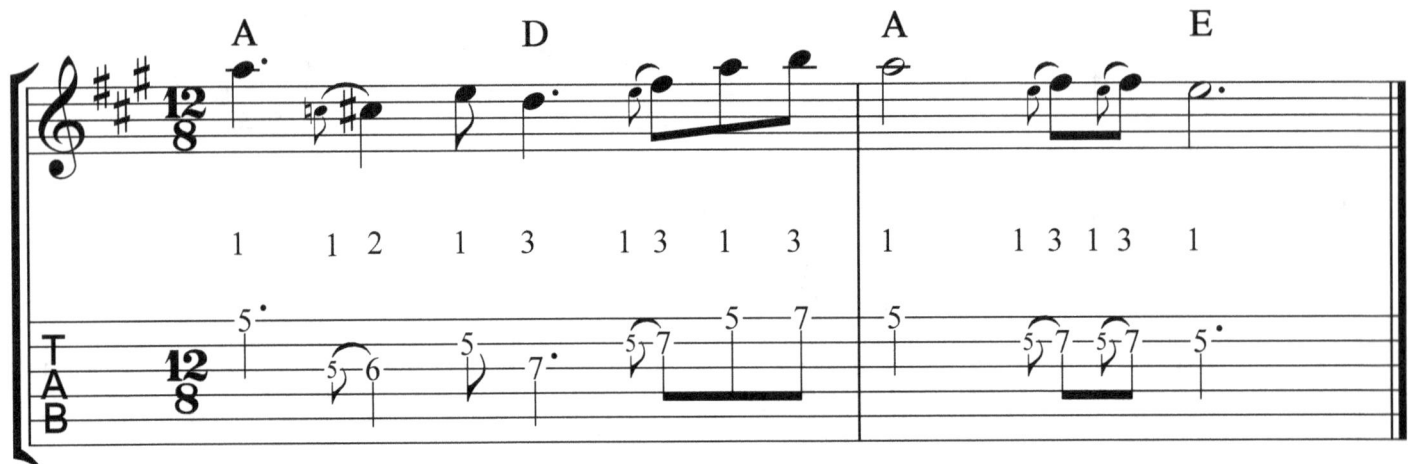

Playing With Jam Track

Play the complete solo along with the jam track, *Key To The A Way* from the *Let's Jam! CD Blues & Rock Volume 3*.

You can access and download the file from the following web address: http://cvls.com/extras/ecs/.

Eric Clapton Style Solo 1

By Jody Worrell

Phrase 1

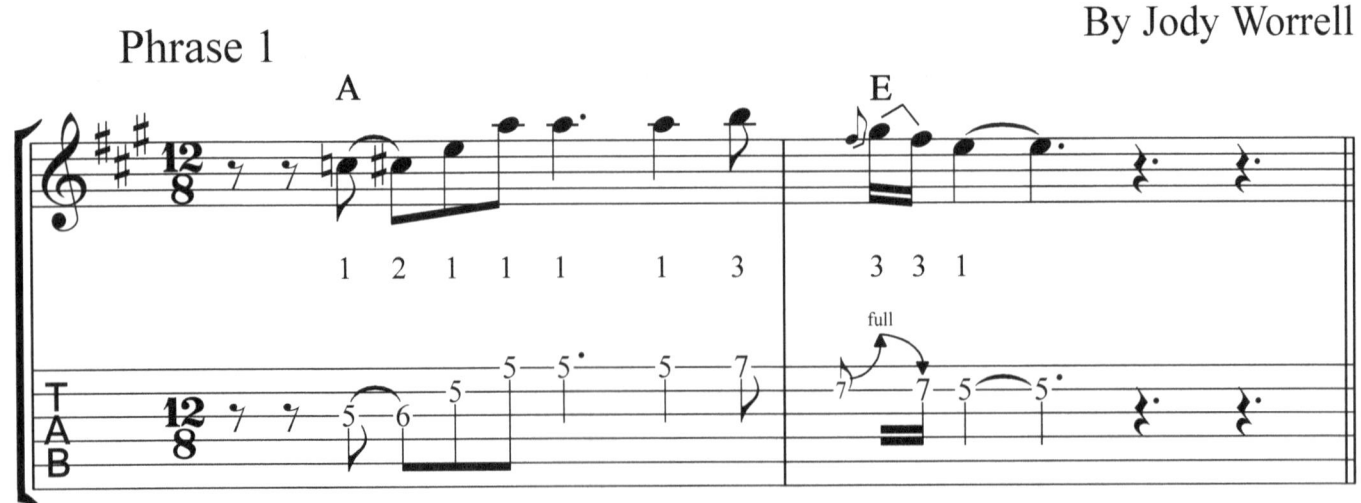

Phrase 2

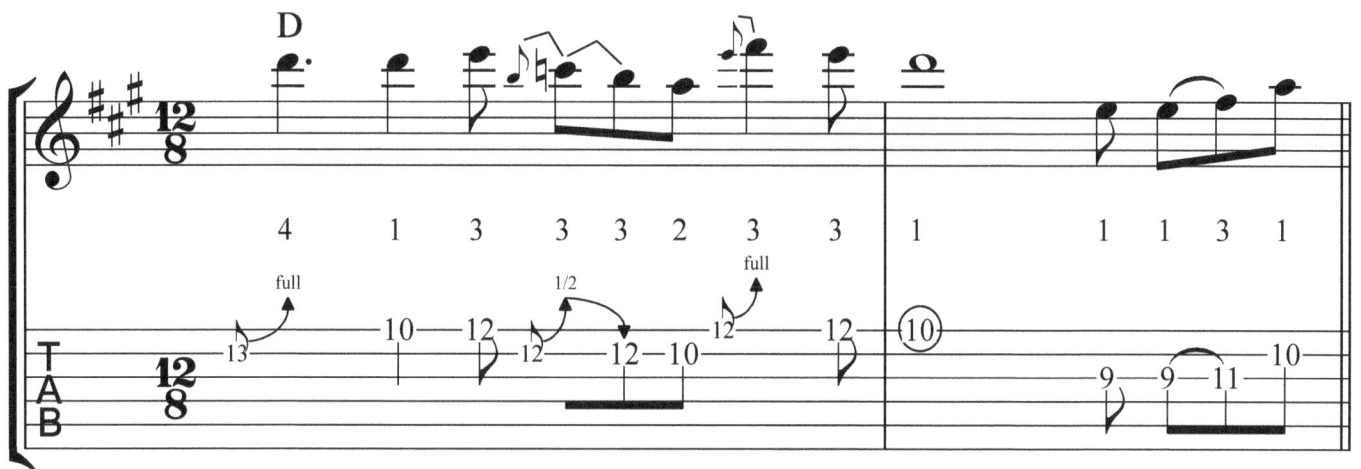

Phrase 3

Phrase 4

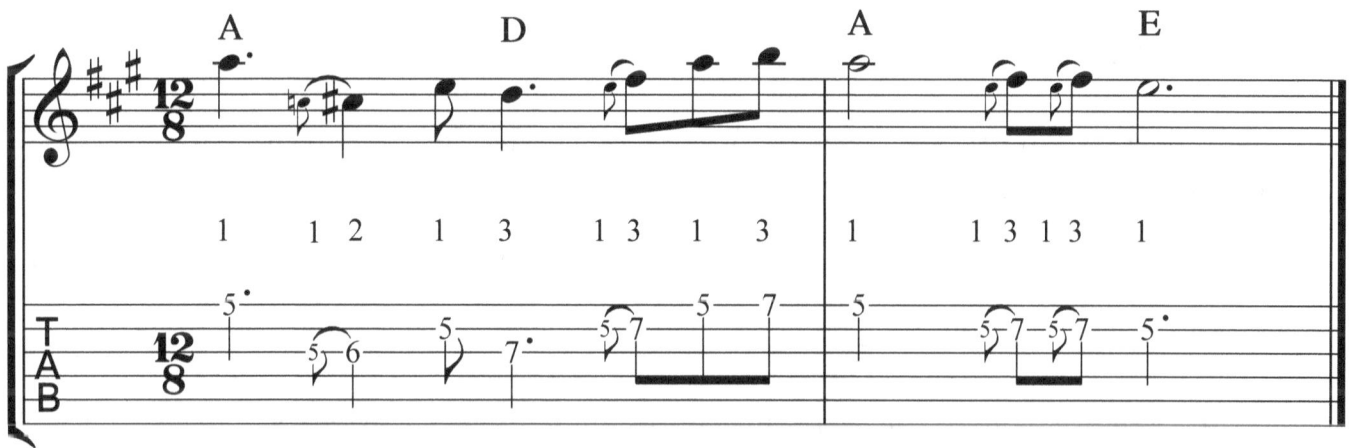

Eric Clapton Style Solo 2

This is a follow up to Solo 1, again playing over a blues shuffle. In addition to learning a great blues solo, I will provide detailed instruction on specific techniques that Eric used to create his signature style.

Phrase 1

This phrase starts with three groups of three notes. You can slide into all three groups if you like.

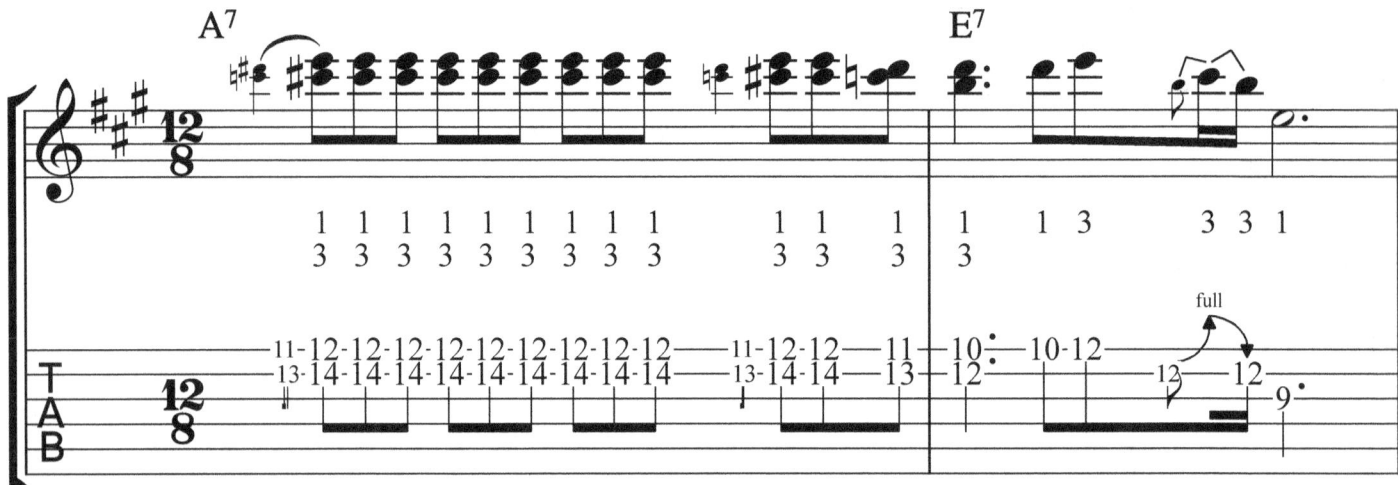

Demo

Each phrase will be played along with a backing track at the correct speed.

Trading Licks

Each lick will be traded back & forth. I'll play it first, then leave space for you to play it right after so you can compare your tone, timing, and articulation. Take your time and work on this section until you can play it perfectly all three times through.

Video & Audio Access

To Access Audio & Video for this course, go to this web address:
http://cvls.com/extras/ecs/

Phrase 2

Play close attention to cutting off the sound of the bends. Listen to the DVD for an explanation.

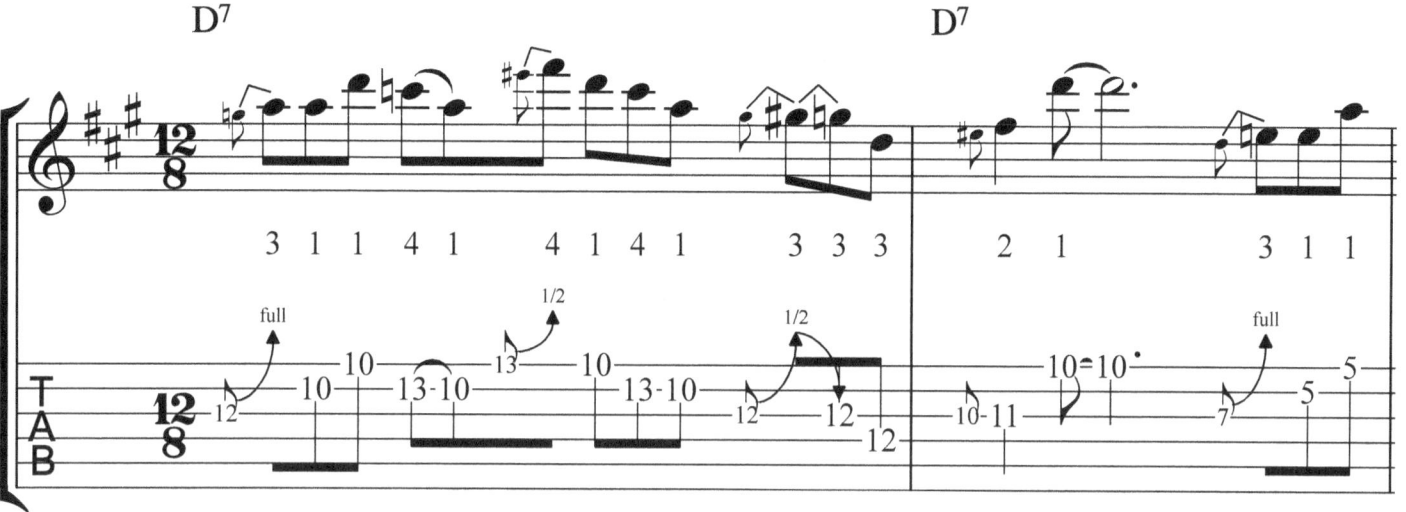

Phrase 3

The last three notes of Phrase 2 are pickup notes for this phrase.

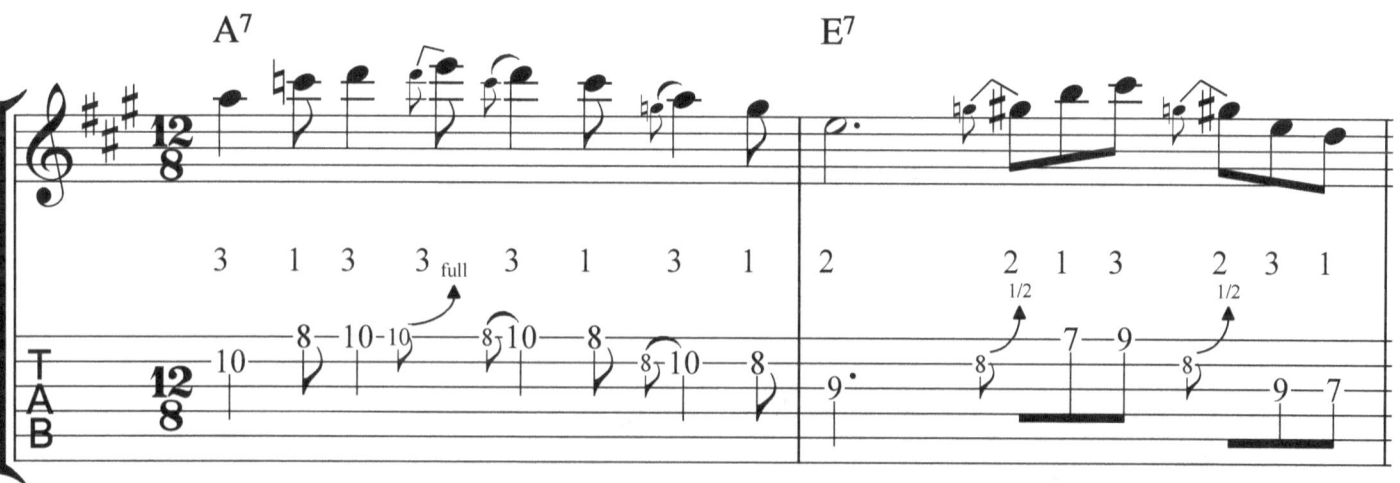

Phrase 4

The last notes from Phrase 3 are also part of this phrase.

Playing With Jam Track

Play the complete solo along with the jam track, *Key To The A Way* from the *Let's Jam! CD Blues & Rock Volume 3*.

To practice along with just the audio track, you can access and download the file from the following web address:
http://cvls.com/extras/ecs/.

Eric Clapton Style Solo 2

Phrase 1   By Jody Worrell

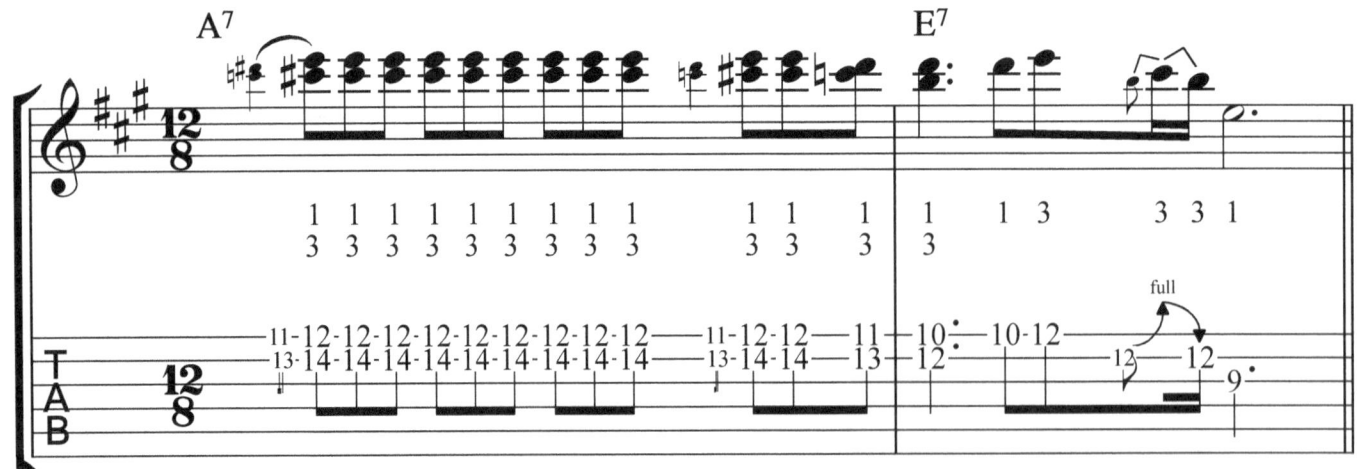

24

Phrase 2

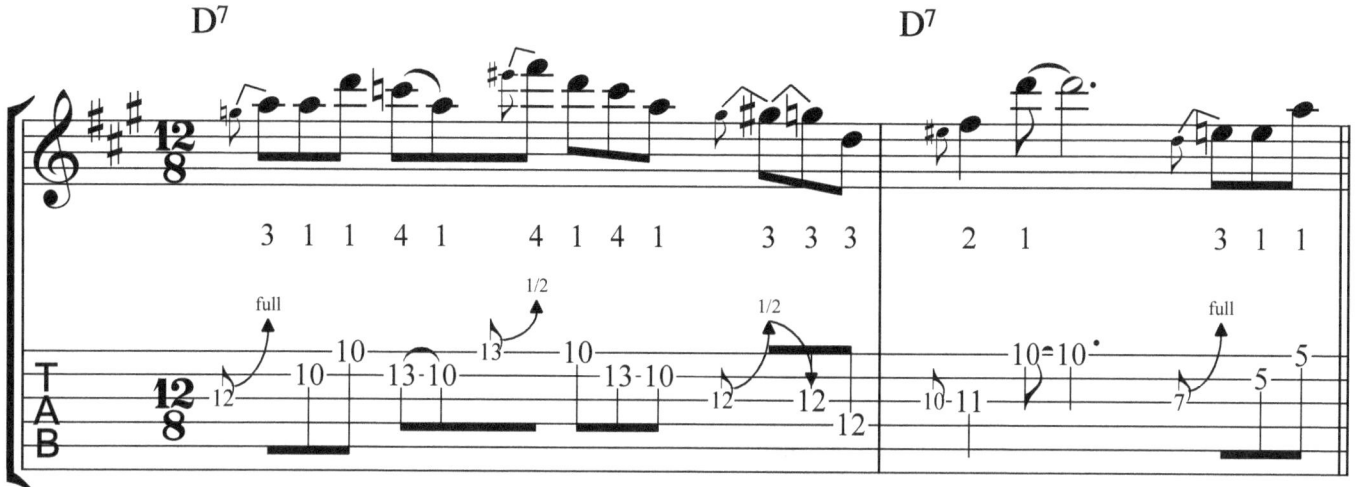

Phrase 3

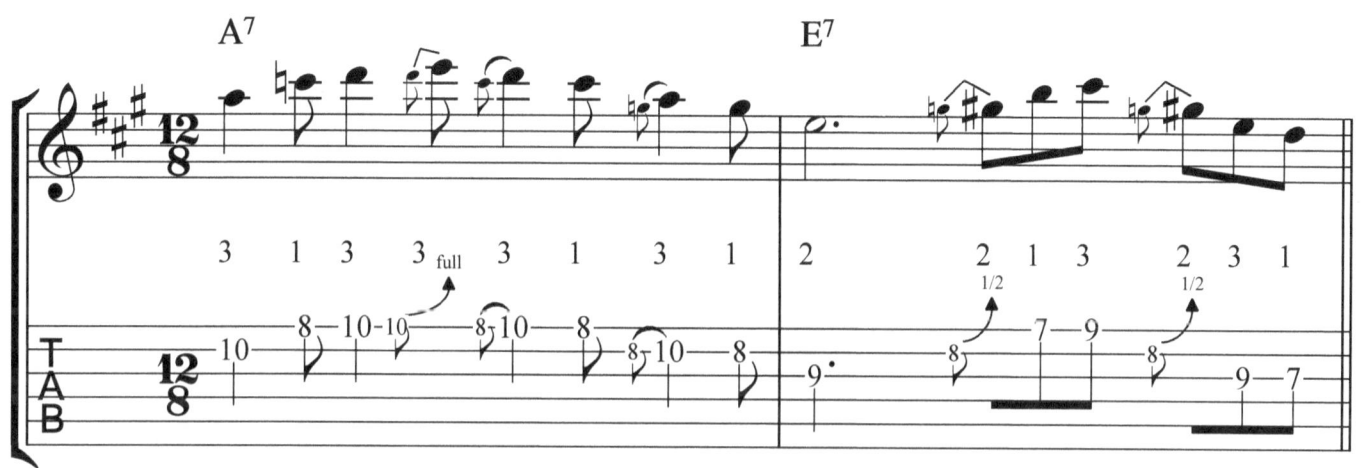

Phrase 4

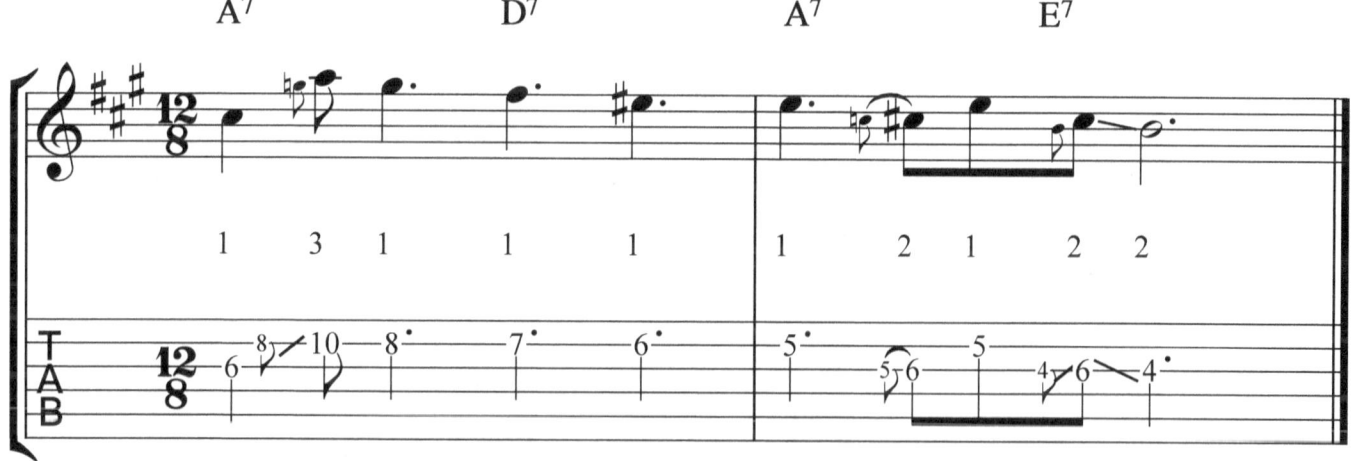

Clapton Style Solo In C 1

This solo will be played over a two chord groove of C7 and F7 in the style of Eric Clapton. I will walk you through playing the solo in detail focusing on Clapton's bending, vibrato, and tone styles. Then I will break down the solo into four smaller sections and explain how to play them in detail. You will get the opportunity to practice each section and the entire solo along with a rhythm track.

Phrase 1

This phrase uses a classic Clapton style slide in the 2nd bar.

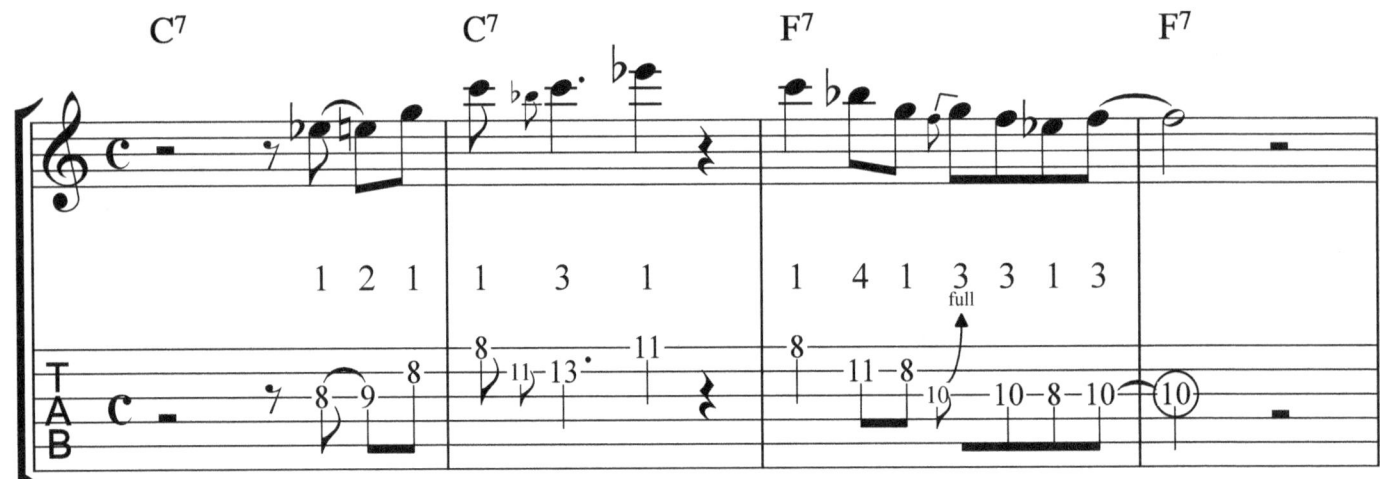

Demo

Each phrase will be played along with a backing track at the correct speed.

Trading Licks

Each lick will be traded back & forth. I'll play it first, then leave space for you to play it right after so you can compare your tone, timing, and articulation. Take your time and work on this section until you can play it perfectly all three times through.

Video & Audio Access

To Access Audio & Video for this course, go to this web address:
http://cvls.com/extras/ecs/

Phrase 2

Phrase 2 uses slides up and down the neck.

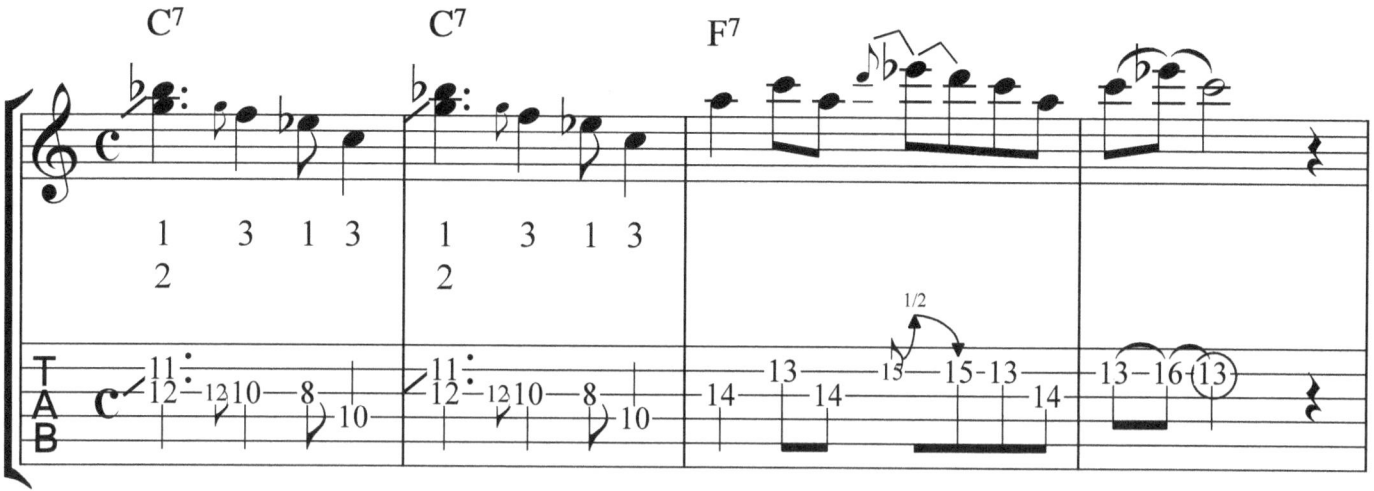

Phrase 3

Move up to the 16th fret for Phrase 3.

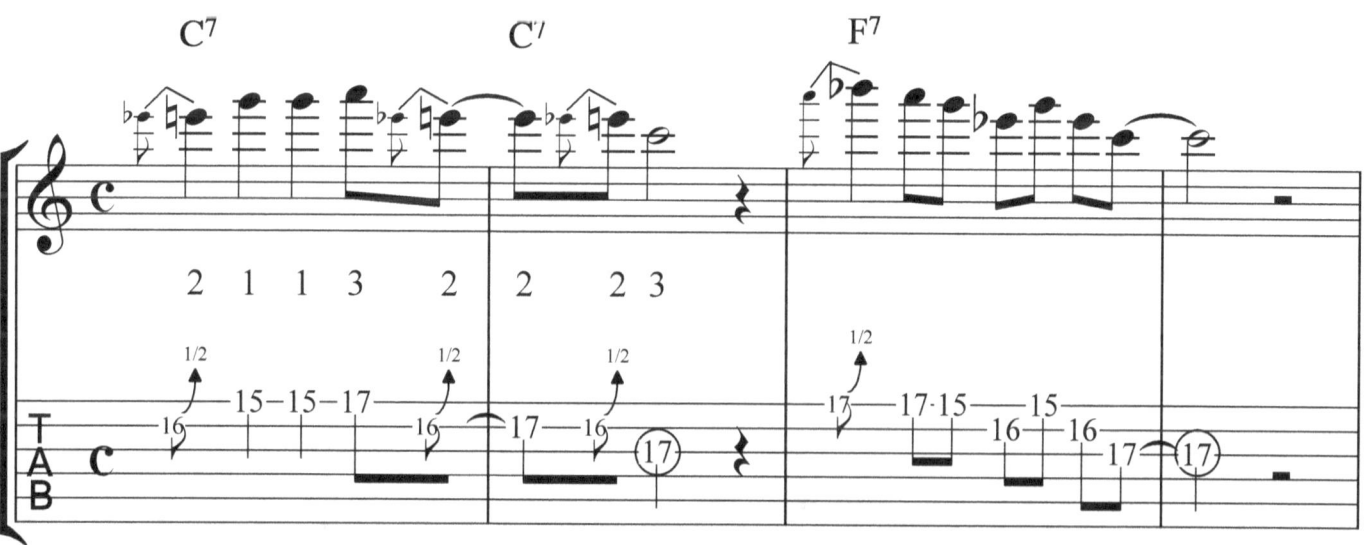

Phrase 4

Phrase 4 uses lots of slides.

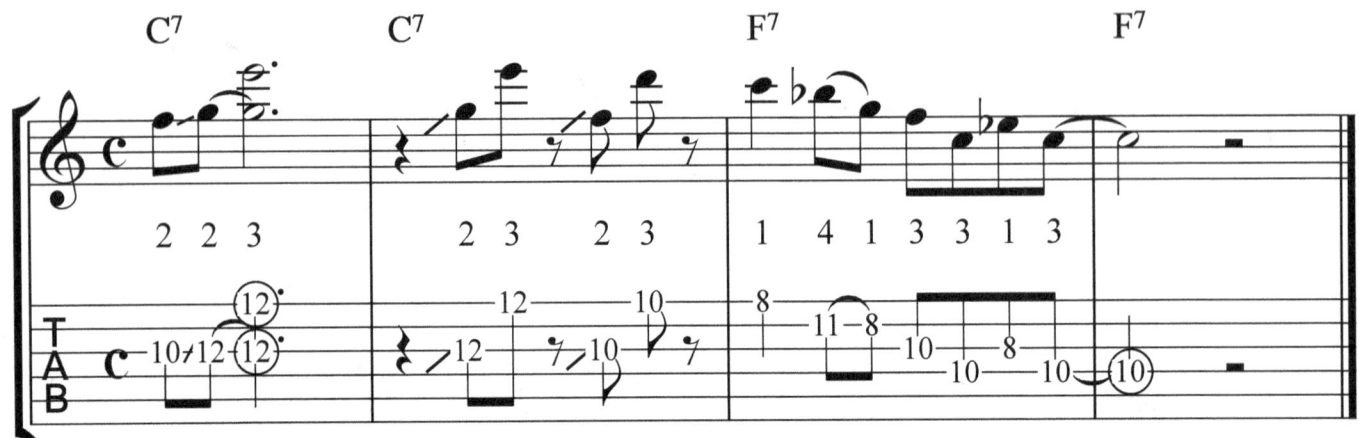

Playing With Jam Track

Play the complete solo along with the jam track, *Over The Weather* from the *Let's Jam! CD Blues & Rock Volume 3*.

To practice along with just the audio track, you can access and download the file from the following web address:
                        http://cvls.com/extras/ecs/

Clapton Style Solo In C 1

By Jody Worrell

Phrase 1

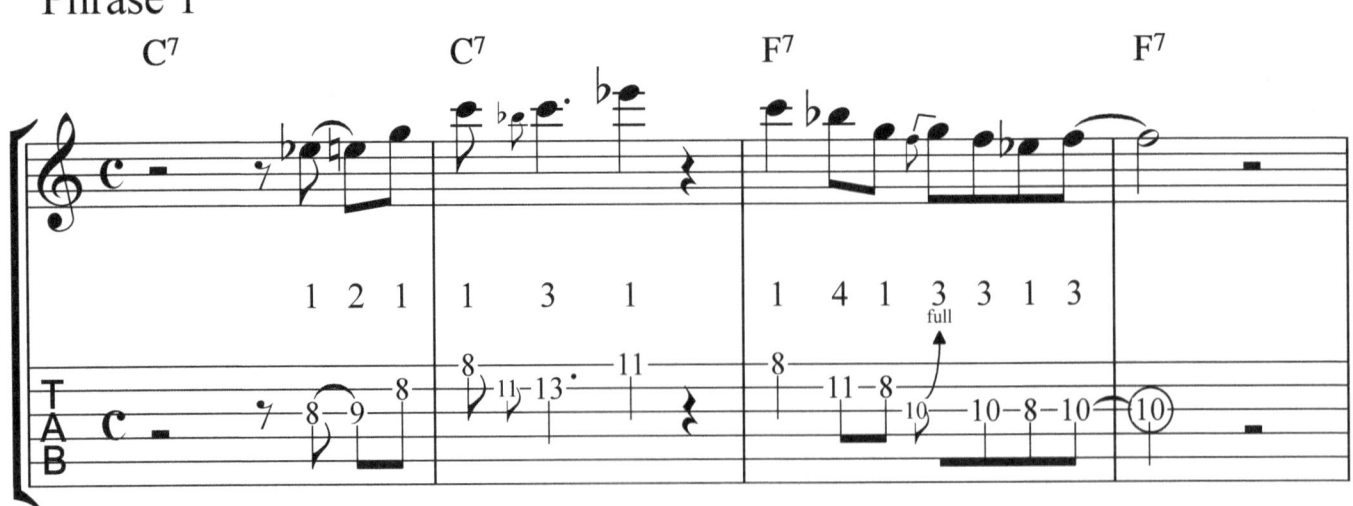

28

Phrase 2
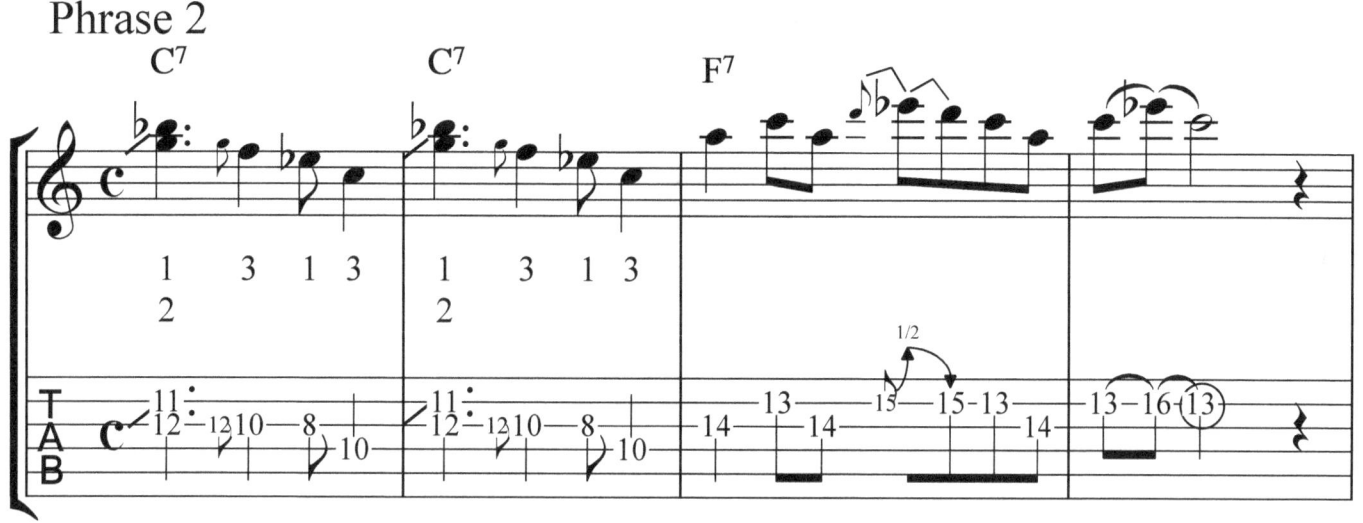

Phrase 3
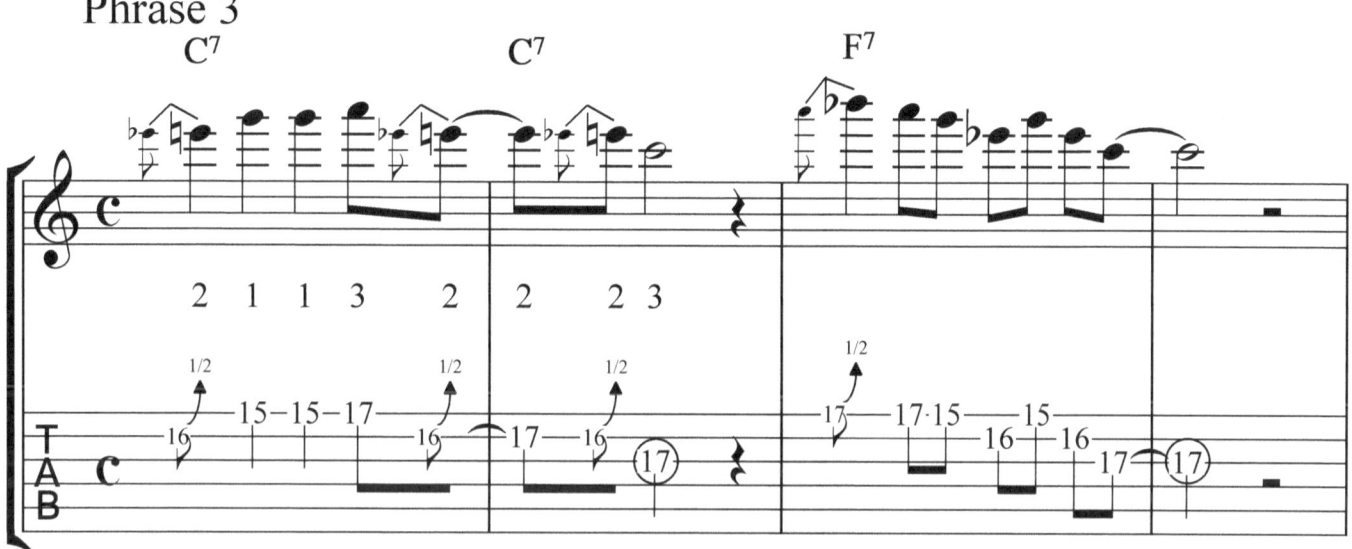

Phrase 4
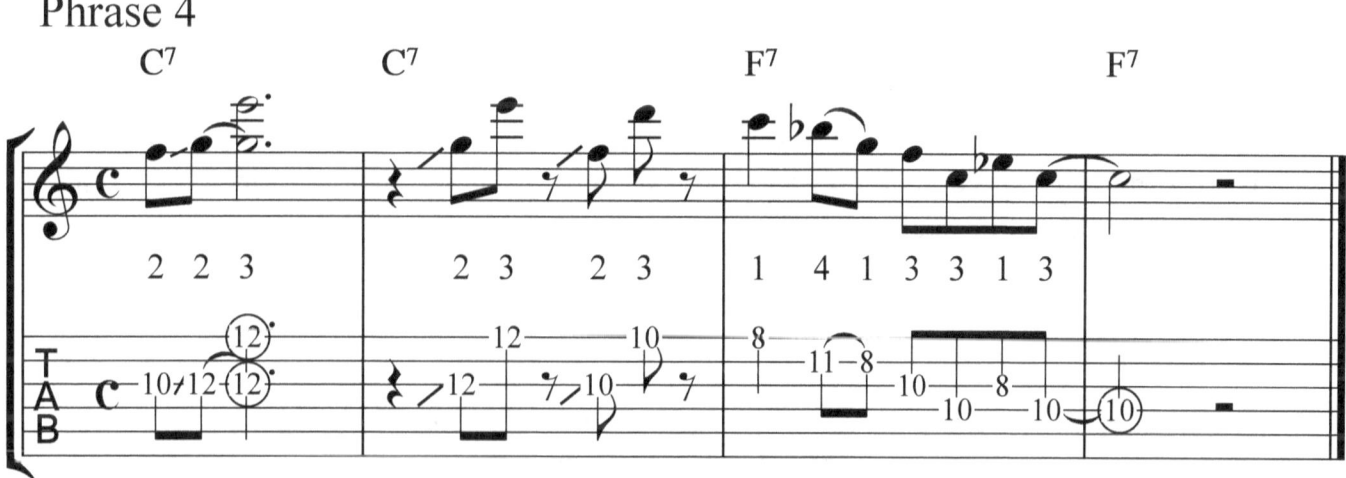

Clapton Style Solo In C 2

This lesson will build on *Solo In C 1* by teaching you another 16 bar blues solo in the key of C. I will break the solo down into four bar sections. You will learn how to play the solo note by note and get to practice with jam tracks that loop each section.

Phrase 1

Phrase 1 uses the major pentatonic scale at the 5th fret.

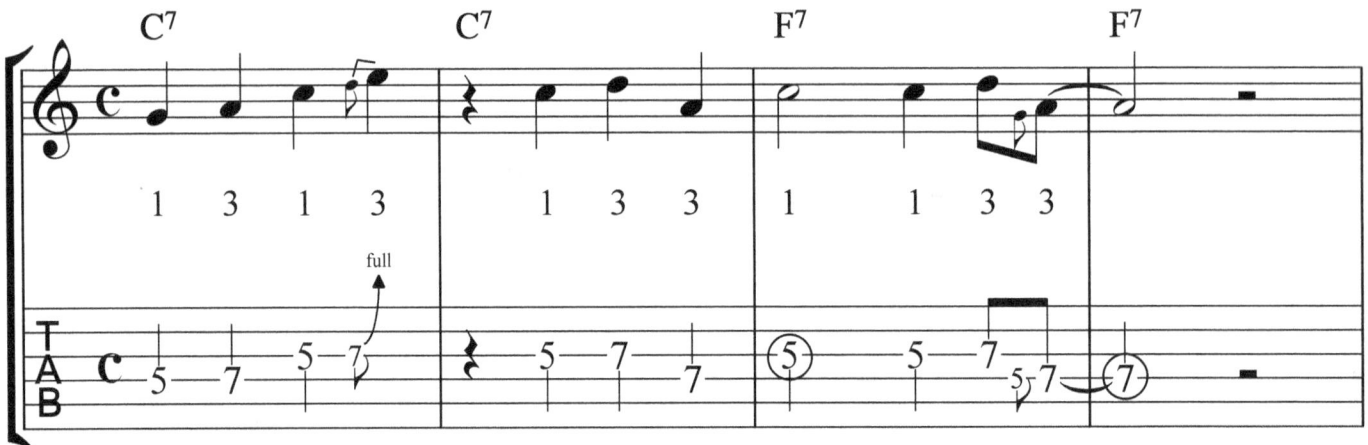

Demo

Each phrase will be played along with a backing track at the correct speed.

Trading Licks

Each lick will be traded back & forth. I'll play it first, then leave space for you to play it right after so you can compare your tone, timing, and articulation. Take your time and work on this section until you can play it perfectly all three times through.

Video & Audio Access

To Access Audio & Video for this course, go to this web address:
http://cvls.com/extras/ecs/

Phrase 2

Phrase 2 moves up the neck.

Phrase 3

Practice muting after bending in the 2nd bar. Listen to the DVD for details.

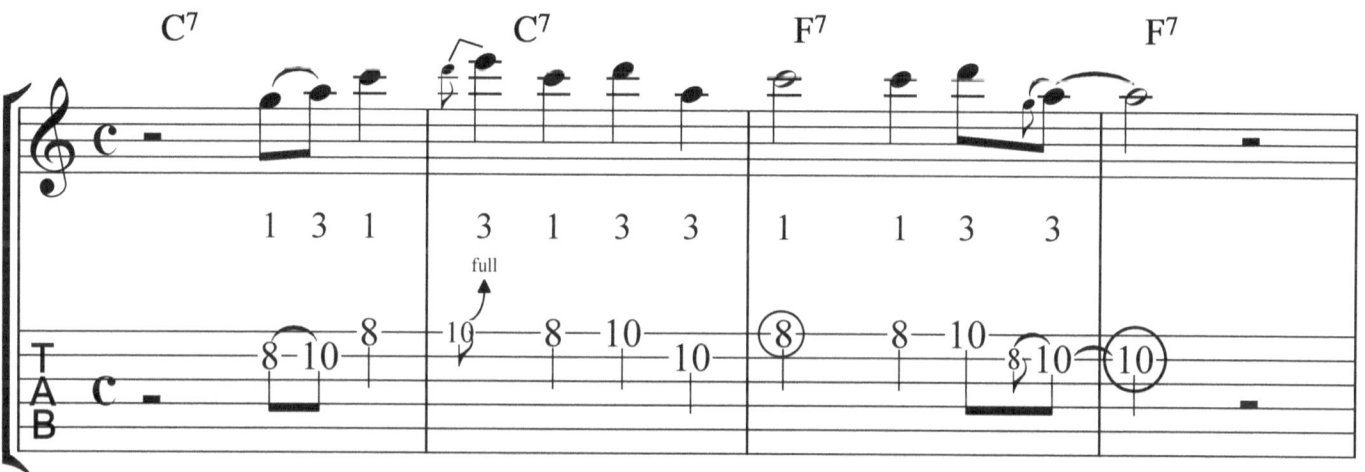

Phrase 4

This phrase uses lots of slides.

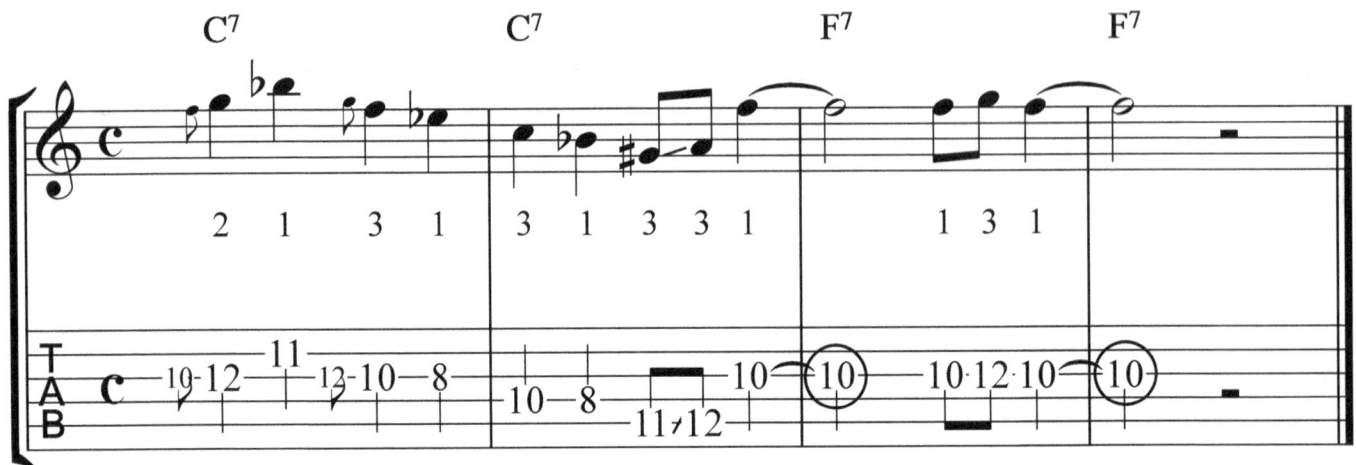

Playing With Jam Track

Play the complete solo along with the jam track, *Over The Weather* from the *Let's Jam! CD Blues & Rock Volume 3*.

To practice along with just the audio track, you can access and download the file from the following web address:

        http://cvls.com/extras/ecs/

Clapton Style Solo In C 2

By Jody Worrell

Phrase 1

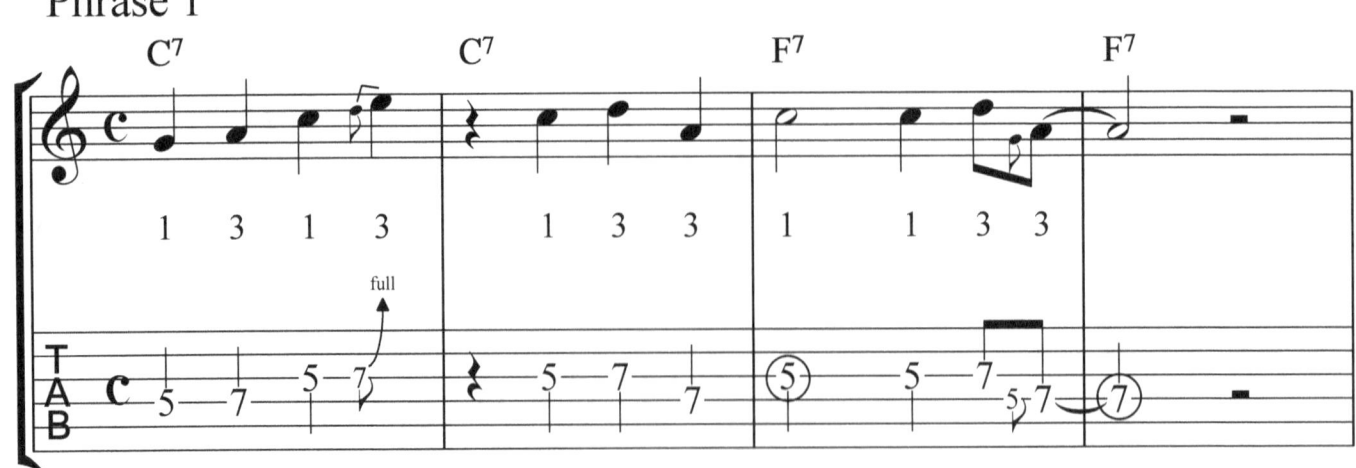

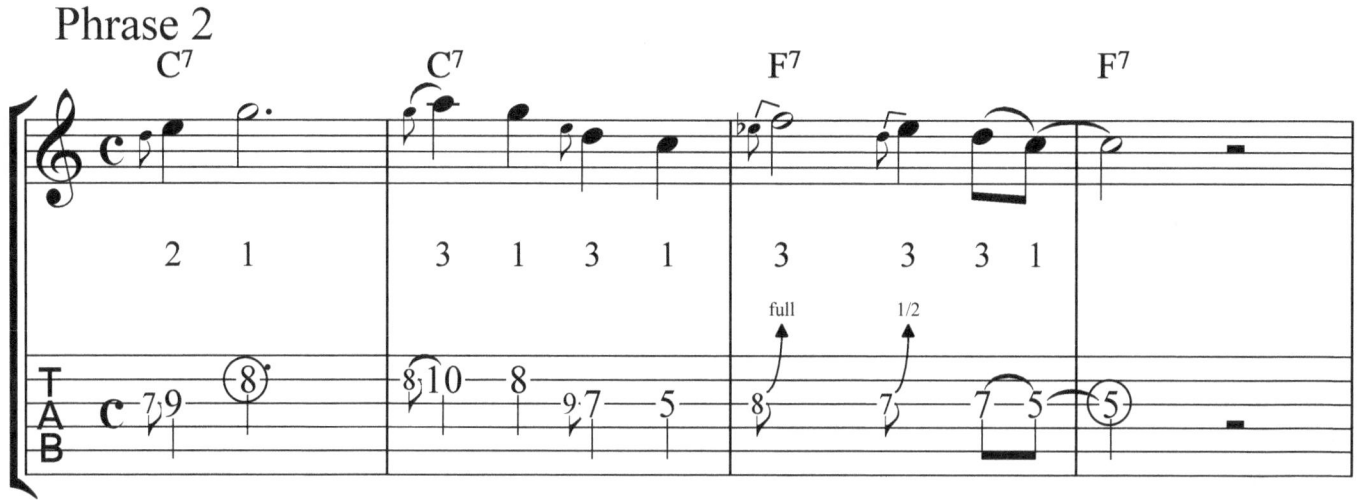
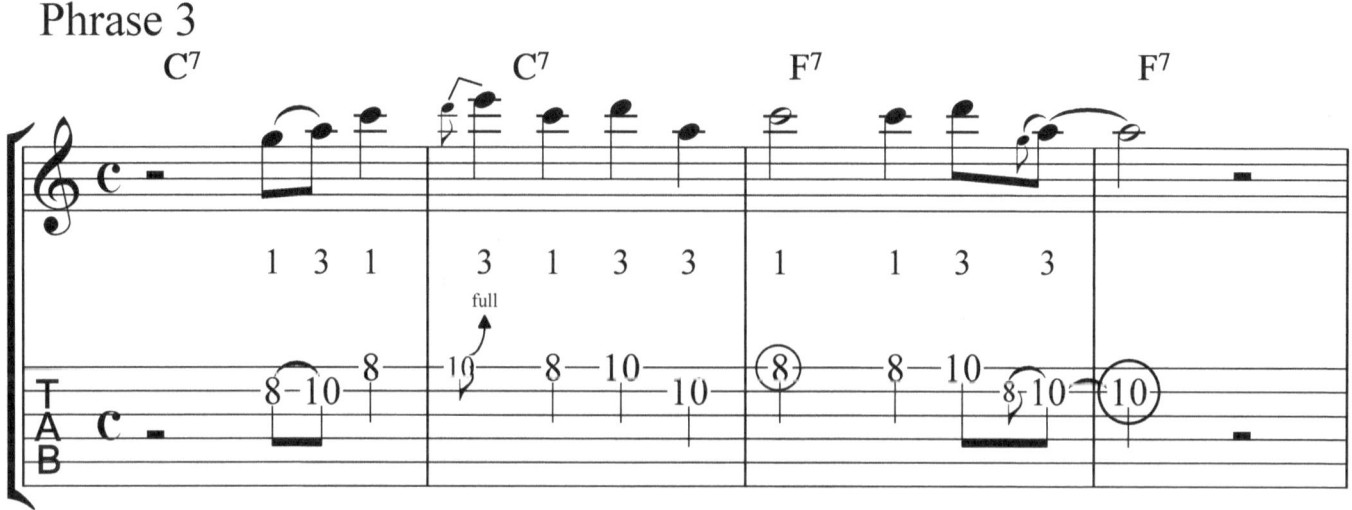
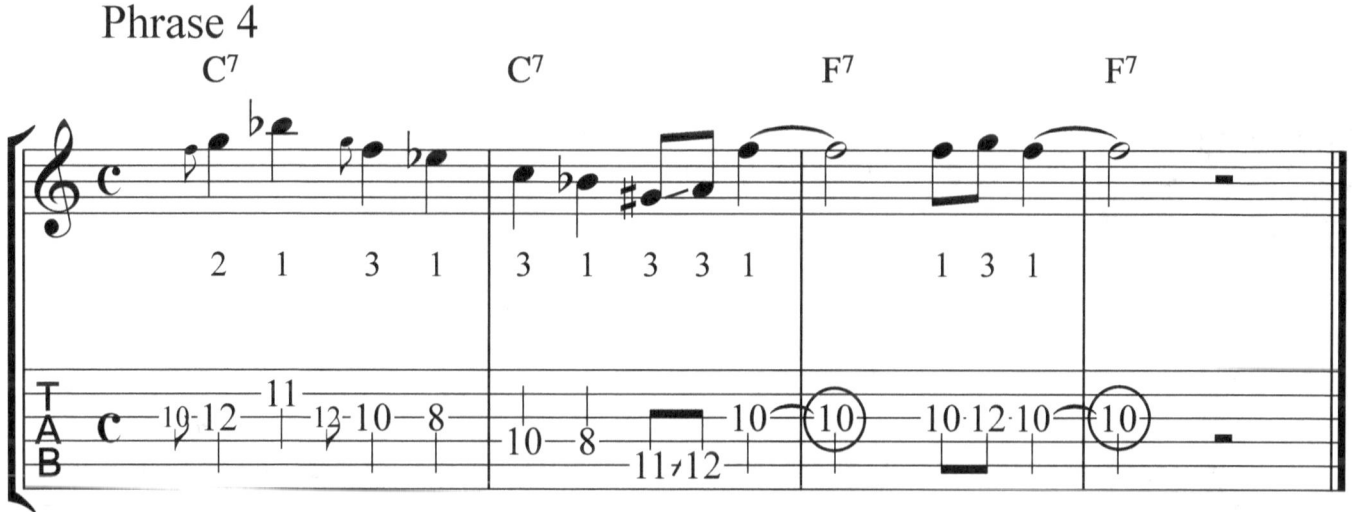

OTHER PRODUCTS IN THIS SERIES

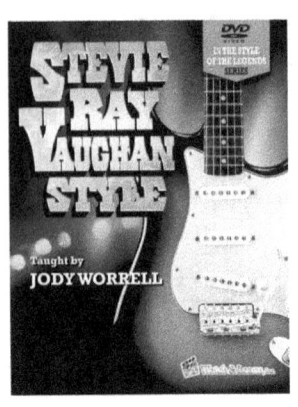

The *Stevie Ray Vaughan Style Guitar Book* by Jody Worrell touches on the techniques and style that helped establish Stevie Ray Vaughan as a legitimate guitar hero. Jody will take you step by step through licks and solos teaching Stevie's approach to bends, slurs, hammer-ons, pull-offs, and note selection. After teaching you the lead parts, Jody will demonstrate them over a rhythm track. The included lessons are Stevie Ray Style Licks in A 1 & 2, Stevie Ray Swing Solos 1 & 2, and Stevie Ray Minor Solos 1 & 2. The package includes guitar tabs, 151 minutes of video instruction, and audio jam tracks.

Jimi Hendrix Style Book by Jody Worrell teaches the techniques and style that helped establish Jimi Hendrixas a legendary guitar hero. You will go step by step through the licks and solos learning Jimi's approach to bends, slides, hammer-ons, pull-offs, and note selection. After learning the lead parts, they will be demonstrated over a full band rhythm track. Each lick or phrase will then be traded back and forth. Jody will play it first and leave room for you to play immediately after. The package includes guitar tabs, over 3 hours of video instruction, and audio jam tracks for each lesson.

B.B. King Style Guitar Book by Jody Worrell teaches the techniques and style that helped establish B.B. King as a blues legend. You will learn the timing, note selection, bends, vibrato, and famous box position that all combine to create B.B.'s unique phrasing. After learning the lead parts, they will be demonstrated over a full band rhythm track. Each lick or phrase will then be traded back and forth. Jody will play it first and leave room for you to play immediately after. The package includes guitar tabs, over 3 hours of video instruction, and audio practice tracks for each lesson.

Pink Floyd Style Book by Jody Worrell teaches the techniques and style that helped establish David Gilmour as a rock legend. You will learn the timing, note selection, bends, and vibrato that all combine to create David's unique phrasing. After learning the lead parts, they will be demonstrated over a full band rhythm track. Each lick or phrase will then be traded back and forth. Jody will play it first and leave room for you to play immediately after. The package includes guitar tab, over 2.7 hours of video instruction, and audio practice tracks for each lesson.

www.ingramcontent.com/pod-product-compliance
Lightning Source LLC
Chambersburg PA
CBHW080024130526
44591CB00036B/2641